START-A-CRAFT

Greeting Cards

Get started in a new craft with easy-to-follow

projects for beginners

SHARON McSWINEY

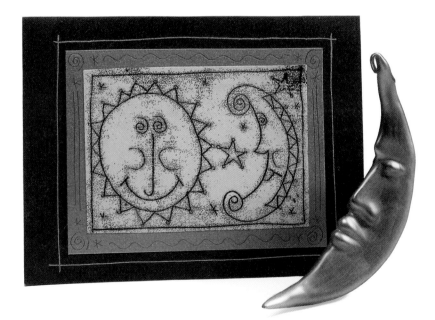

CHARTWELL
BOOKS, INC.

CONTENTS

Introduction **4**

Materials and Equipment **5**

Techniques **9**

Cards from Nature **13**

Spray Stencils **15**

Fabric Trimmings **18**

Monoprinting **20**

Wax Resist **22**

Rubbings **24**

Cards using Metal **26**

Fabric Collage **29**

Stamping **32**

Paint Stencils **34**

Brown Paper Technique **37**

Paper Collage **40**

Natural Prints and Stencils **43**

Envelopes **46**

Suppliers **48**

INTRODUCTION

A handmade card is like a miniature work of art. It will often be kept and framed as an original picture. People tend to appreciate receiving a handmade card that little bit more, as they are more personal than a mass-produced, printed card. Many contemporary craft workers and artists produce their own greeting cards either to give to friends and relatives or very often to sell. I have been making my own cards for several years now: once you start you never look back. I am a person who likes instant results. Enthused by an idea I want to try it out immediately. Making greeting cards enables you to do this. The scale is small and the techniques are often very simple to master. Without any training in art it is possible to produce something very professional in appearance. Many of the techniques illustrated in this book require nothing more than a pot of paint, a crayon or a pen and your imagination. I often use sponges or my fingers rather than brushes. By experimenting a lot, my designs often evolve as I explore different techniques. Many of the techniques in this book adapt for multiple use enabling you to produce many cards at a time, others are more involved to make a very special individual greeting card. This book will show you how to design and create your own greeting cards, some for specific occasions such as Christmas, Birthdays, Weddings, in addition to cards suitable for everyday use.

MATERIALS AND EQUIPMENT

PAINTS AND INKS

DESIGNER GOUACHE:
POSTER COLOR

Available in tubes or small pots it is similar to watercolor paint and is water-soluble. It gives an even matt finish, is fast drying and easily mixed, although a huge spectrum of colors is offered. Readily available from art and good stationery stores.

ORNAMENTAL SPRAY:
METALLIC SILVER AND GOLD SPRAY PAINTS AND AUTOMOBILE SPRAY PAINTS

Hardware stores, art stores and automobile repair stores will stock this type of paint which is available in cans. Use in a "spray booth" in a well ventilated area. It may require practice to avoid applying too much paint at a time.

BLOCK PRINTING INK

Water-soluble, this ink is available in tubes. Use it straight from the tube, there is no need to dilute with water. It is also available oil-based but this takes a much longer period of time to dry. Offered in various colors, although we found black to be the most successful, it is available from art stores.

DRAWING INK

Available in small bottles or jars and water-soluble, it can be used with brushes (wash immediately after use) or steel-nib pens. Various colors are available including metallic gold and silver. It can be bought from art or craft stores.

WAX CRAYONS AND CANDLES

Easily available from arts shops and stationery stores. Crayons intended for children are ideal, as they are inexpensive, non-toxic and available in a variety of colors and sizes. Household candles can be used to good effect as a resist material.

PENS AND PENCILS

A selection of different pens will be useful such as; a permanent fineline drawing pen (¼in or ⅛in), a black water-soluble marker pen, a fiber-tip pen plus gold and silver fineline metallic marker pens. A general purpose HB pencil is required, a softer 4B pencil for transferring designs and a range of inexpensive colored pencils will also be useful for adding smaller details to artwork.

ADHESIVES

GLUE-STICK

A solid block of adhesive in a stick form is useful for bonding most types of paper. When only a small amount of adhesive is required in a particular area it is easy to control the amount of glue applied to the paper.

CLEAR STRONG ADHESIVE

Available in tubes this adhesive is required for sticking thicker papers and card. It is also useful for attaching non-paper items. Use in a well ventilated area and protect your work surface.

ALL-PURPOSE ADHESIVE OR PVA

A white non-toxic water-based glue which dries clear and is available in plastic bottles. Any excess glue can be removed by gently rubbing it off the paper. It can be applied with a brush, but it must be rinsed out with water immediately after use. Suitable for bonding fabrics. It can also be diluted, if required, for fine fabrics.

DOUBLE-SIDED ADHESIVE TAPE

A useful alternative to glue which gives a strong bond. It can be cut into small sections and placed exactly where required and will attach quite heavy card and non-paper items.

MASKING TAPE

A tape which can easily be removed from most surfaces without damaging them. Therefore it is very useful for temporarily securing items such as stencils.

TOOLS

CUTTING MAT

This synthetic mat, made from a dense plastic, allows you to cut into it many times without damage. Useful for general cutting and intricate work, it can be quite an expensive purchase if not used regularly. A thick piece of cardboard could be substituted.

SCALPEL AND CRAFT KNIFE

A craft knife with snap-off blades ensures you always have a sharp cutting tool. Useful for general cutting of card. For more intricate work, scalpels are available from art stores. However the blades are very sharp and care should be taken when using them. A cork is a good way to protect the blade when not in use.

SCISSORS

It is worthwhile investing in a good pair of general-purpose scissors which will last you for many years. A pair used specifically for cutting fabrics is also required as paper will blunt the scissors very quickly.

STEEL RULER

This is essential for an accurate cutting edge when using a craft knife and is more durable than plastic or wooden rulers.

METAL TINSNIPS

These are available from specialist jewelry tool-stores or good hardware stores and are required for cutting metal. If they are not going to be used regularly, a sharp pair of household scissors could be substituted.

METAL SCRIBER

Used for scribing designs into metal, this will give you a sharp image. However an old ballpoint pen could be used as an alternative.

ARTIST BRUSHES

Available from art stores they come in a variety of different qualities and sizes. Good sable brushes can be very expensive so we suggest a sable/synthetic blend brush (size 7) as suitable for most work. If looked after a brush will last you many years.

STENCIL BRUSHES

These are especially made for stenciling. Available in a variety of sizes and types they have short thick handles and the bristles are cut off flat. Available from good art and craft stores.

ROLLERS

Required for spreading printing ink evenly over a printing surface these are available from art stores in a variety of sizes. Wash immediately after use with warm water or mineral spirit if using oil-based ink.

PAPER AND CARD

A huge range of card and paper is available from art and craft stores. Collect a range of colors, weights and textures. Sugar paper, "Ingres" and cartridge papers are all useful and come in a wide spectrum of colors. An inexpensive watercolor paper is essential for some of the projects in this book. It has the advantage of being able to withstand quantities of water without the paper breaking down and often has a slight texture which can be utilized. Other useful papers and card to obtain are brown parcel paper, tissue paper, foil, thin detail paper, gold and silver card, mounting board, inexpensive cardboard and any unusually textured or handmade papers.

For the large majority of the projects in this book we have used pre-cut card blanks. These are supplied cut and scored in a variety of sizes, colors and types of card and are useful when producing a quantity of cards. They are available from specialist craft suppliers listed on page 48. Alternatively you can cut your own cards from a medium weight of card. It needs to be heavy enough to stand up but not too thick to fold neatly.

TECHNIQUES

CARDS FROM NATURE

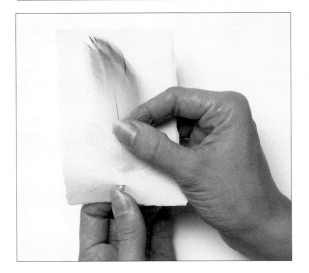

This technique simply involves assembling together feathers, leaves, seed pods, etc, and mounting them onto natural-colored or unusual handmade papers. The paper can be crumpled to give the effect of a dried leaf. Groups of smaller items, such as seed pods, could be mounted together. Larger or more 3D objects require attaching to the paper with glue.

SPRAY STENCILS

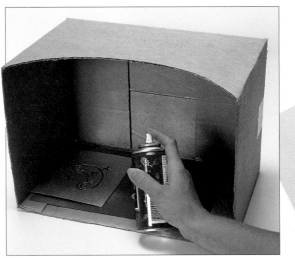

With cardboard and spray paint you can produce a simple stencil which can be used many times. A design is cut from card with a craft knife then ornamental gold or silver paint is then applied over the stencil. An alternative to these paints would be colored automobile lacquer spray paints.

FABRIC TRIMMINGS

With fabric braids, trimmings, and ribbons it is possible to create very effective textured greeting cards. Select unusual braids, cut them to size and paste them onto cards with glue. Combine different sizes and styles for the best results.

MONOPRINTING

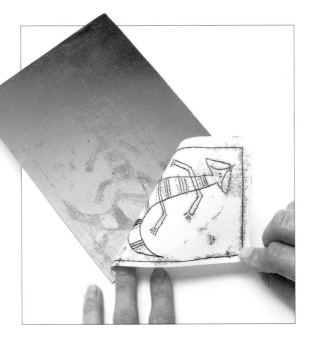

With this simple technique you can produce "one-off" prints. Linear designs are most suitable, although tone could be added by applying pressure with your fingers to specific areas.

Spread a small amount of block printing ink over a flat surface using rollers. This surface could be a marble slab, perspex, or glass. (The glass from clip frames is very suitable as there are no sharp edges.)

Once the ink is evenly distributed over the surface place a sheet of paper in top. For the best results use a smooth paper. If the paper is too textured it will affect the amount of ink picked up. A design is then drawn onto the paper with a pen or pencil remembering that the print will be the reverse of the drawn image. You could also experiment making marks and patterns with alternative items instead of a pen or pencil such as forks, knitting needles, corks, or chop sticks! When the design is complete, the paper is carefully peeled back to reveal the monoprint and left to dry.

WAX RESIST

By using a wax crayon or household candle as a resist material you can create unusual effects on paper with paints. Designs are drawn onto watercolor paper with the candle and a color wash is then applied with gouache. The paint will not adhere to the wax surface.

CARDS USING METAL

This is an interesting method of using empty aluminum drink cans. The can must be aluminum and not steel. You can check this by using a magnet as it will not stick to aluminum. Steel cans are too springy for this project, the aluminum is softer and easier to work with. The can is cut up into small sections using metal snips. Designs can be "drawn" into the metal surface using a scriber. Initially you will find that straight lines are easier to manage than curved, however with practice you can gain more control of the scriber.

RUBBINGS

A "master" is made in paper from which rubbings are taken using a wax crayon and some thin detail paper. A design is cut out from cartridge paper or similar, and built up in layers to create a textured surface. This process may take some time but once you have made the "tool" the rubbing process is very quick. Check your design as you stick each section by making trial rubbings. Thin paper works best to rub onto, you could also try tissue paper. Various colors can be added by successive rubbings. Rub the crayon gently over the surface in all directions, having secured the paper to the "master" with masking tape.

FABRIC COLLAGE

A collection of small fabric scrap pieces can be transformed into a very special greeting card by building up layers of different fabrics. A simple motif, such as a heart, star, or flower forms the center piece of the collage. This is cut from felt fabric, stitched onto a backing and given a 3D effect by padding with cotton balls. This is then sewn to a background fabric and layers are built up using PVA glue to complete the effect.

PAINT STENCILS

A stencil is produced from acetate sheet for this technique. This allows fine details to be cut and the stencil is quite long lasting. A design is cut out of the acetate using a scalpel which is easier to manipulate than a craft knife especially when removing small sections from a design. When complete the stencil is secured to paper with masking tape. Paint, such as gouache, is applied with a special stencil brush and stippled over the whole surface of the stencil.

Alternatives to stencil brushes can be used such as sponges, cloths, or artist brushes. The tape is then removed and the stencil lifted to reveal the printed motif. The process can be repeated several times if required. Different colored paints could be used or combined on one stencil. Gold or silver ink would embellish the design as a final layer on top of the paint.

STAMPING

This technique enables you to make repeat patterns. A simple stamping tool is made from a cork; large corks such as Champagne corks are most suitable for this as they are easier to hold and the actual cork material is more dense and will hold the design better. The motif is cut into the end of the cork surface with a scalpel or craft knife. This tool can be used with inks or paints to produce almost limitless prints. Interesting patterns are made by the cork surface itself, each cork creating a unique type of print.

BROWN PAPER TECHNIQUE

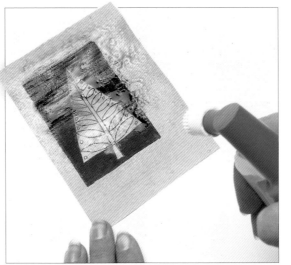

Using brown parcel paper and a combination of both waterproof and water-soluble pens, it is possible to create a unique "one-off" image. A design is first drawn with a black fineline permanent pen and then the surrounding area is filled in with a water-soluble black marker pen. The ink is made to "bleed" by a fine mist of water from a water spray. This often causes different colors to appear from the black. When dry, touches of gold or silver ink complete the effect.

NATURAL PRINTS AND STENCILS

This involves using leaves to print from and as stencils. Paint is applied directly onto the surface of a leaf. A print is then made from it by placing the leaf between two sheets of paper and gently rubbing over the surface. This can be repeated if required by applying more paint. The paper is then peeled back to reveal the print. Leaves can also be utilized to create an interesting background for the print. Place a selection onto a sheet of paper and spray over the whole area with ornamental spray. The leaves are then removed to reveal a silhouette of their image.

PAPER COLLAGE

By combining painted paper surfaces and foil papers you can produce highly individual collages. A background is made by applying gouache paint to watercolor paper with sponges rather than paint brushes. By then misting this surface with water the painted areas merge together. Gold or silver ink is then dripped over the surface. When dry, layers of foil papers are applied to give a rich effect.

ENVELOPES

You may wish to make your own envelopes rather than use those commercially produced. The basic principle involves selecting a large piece of paper, measuring around your folded card and adding on a ¼ in border. From this you measure diagonally from the corners to find the center. Measure to the top and bottom edges, add ½ in for an overlap and draw lines up to meet these points. Repeat the process for the side flaps but there is no need to add the extra ½ in. Cut out and apply a small amount of glue to the bottom flap to assemble the envelope.

OTHER TECHNIQUES

TRANSFERRING A DESIGN

Using tracing paper, draw out the design with an HB pencil. When complete turn over the paper and rub over the whole area with a soft 4B pencil. Place the tracing paper in position on the selected paper, right side up, and go over the lines with the HB pencil. The design will be transferred onto the paper.

CARDS FROM NATURE

A simple method of producing a unique greeting card is to collect feathers, leaves in fall, seed pods or dried flowers and mount them onto textured, natural-colored papers. Handmade papers are also available, many of which would complement the natural objects used.

You will need

◊ A feather; chicken or duck feathers are very suitable

◊ Sugar paper in 2 colors; pale beige and pink (8¼ × 11⅓in)

◊ Natural color card blank; 6 × 8in

◊ Pair of scissors

◊ Craft knife

◊ Masking tape

◊ Cutting mat

TIP

• When using dried leaves, seed pods etc mount them using PVA glue and leave to dry for 30–40 minutes.

1 Select your feather and its background paper. Carefully tear the paper to the correct size. A torn edge will give a more interesting effect.

2 Place the backing paper on the cutting mat and with a craft knife, make two slits in the paper.

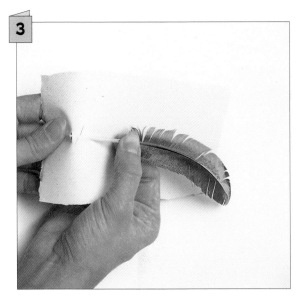

3 Slide the shaft of the feather through the slits until the feather lies in the desired position on the paper.

4 Turn over the paper and keeping the feather in position put a piece of tape over the openings and the feather shaft to secure the feather in place.

5

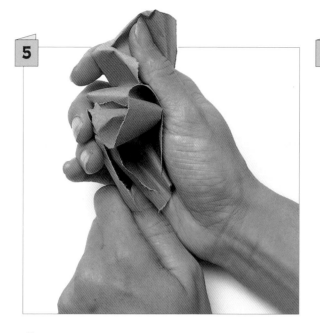

5 To further decorate the card, select a complementary colored paper for a background. Crumple this sheet of paper in your hands.

6

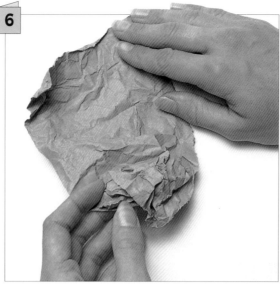

6 Flatten out the paper, then tear it to size. Apply glue, then stick this to a larger folded, contrasting card.

7

7 To complete the greeting card, glue the paper holding the feather onto the middle of the crumpled effect background paper.

TIP

• Skeleton leaves can be bought from florists.

SPRAY STENCILS

This quick and easy method of producing a stencil from card can be used many times to create a repeated image or to make multiples of the same card. For this project we have used a simple Christmas tree motif.

You will need

◊ Piece of card; ⅟₁₆in thickness, 3½ × 4¾in
◊ Cutting mat
◊ Craft knife
◊ HB pencil
◊ Gold ornamental spray paint
◊ Fineline gold marker pen
◊ Bright red cartridge paper
◊ Dark green card blank, 4 x 6in

1 Draw the Christmas tree motif onto card, making sure that at least a ¾in space surrounds the design.

2 Place the card on a cutting mat. Carefully cut out the different sections of the design with a craft knife, and then remove them.

TIP

• To protect the surrounding area when spraying, construct a "spray booth" from a cardboard box. Always spray in a well ventilated area; preferably outside if possible.

TIP

• The stencil can be sprayed several times to produce an overlaid effect.

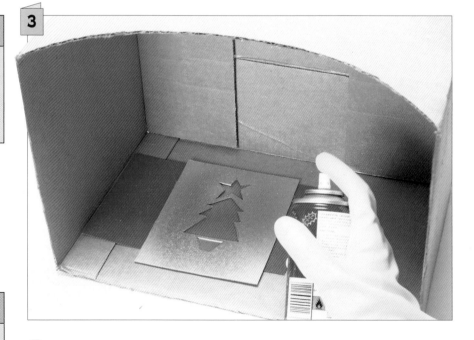

3 Once you have done this, place the stencil on top of the selected paper. Spray paint over the stencil in a simple "spray booth".

4

4 Once the paint is dry, after approximately five minutes, tear the paper to size.

5

5 Draw further decorative elements on the paper with a gold or silver pen to complete the design.

6

6 Take the piece of paper with the design on it, and glue it onto the front of a larger contrasting colored card, which has been folded in half.

7

7 To add a finishing touch to your greeting card, draw a gold border along the edges of the contrasting card.

FABRIC TRIMMINGS

By using fabric braids and trimmings you can create unusually textured cards. Collect "off-cuts" or buy a few special braids. It is a good idea to decide upon a color "theme". Here we have used rich reds and golds.

1 Choose the different braids which you want to use and cut them to size.

You will need
◊ Three different types of braids
◊ PVA adhesive
◊ An old paint brush
◊ Fabric cutting scissors
◊ Deep red card blank, 4 × 6in

2 Arrange the braids in the pattern you want on the folded card before sticking them down. Apply glue to the back of the pieces and then stick them directly onto the card surface.

3

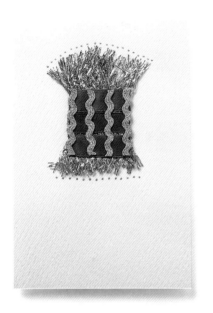

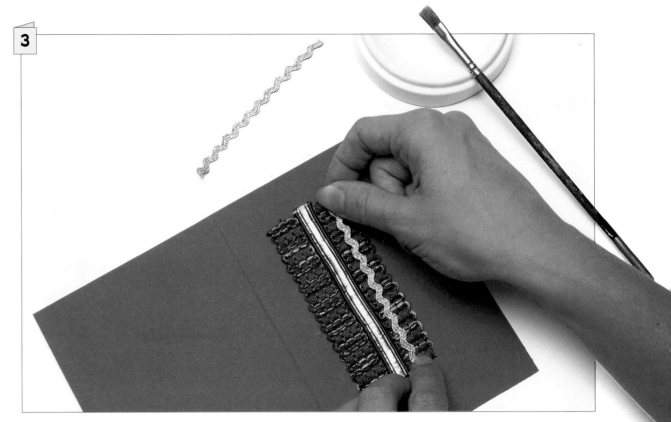

3 Build up layers of different colors and textures to complete the pattern. Leave the card to dry for approximately 50–60 minutes.

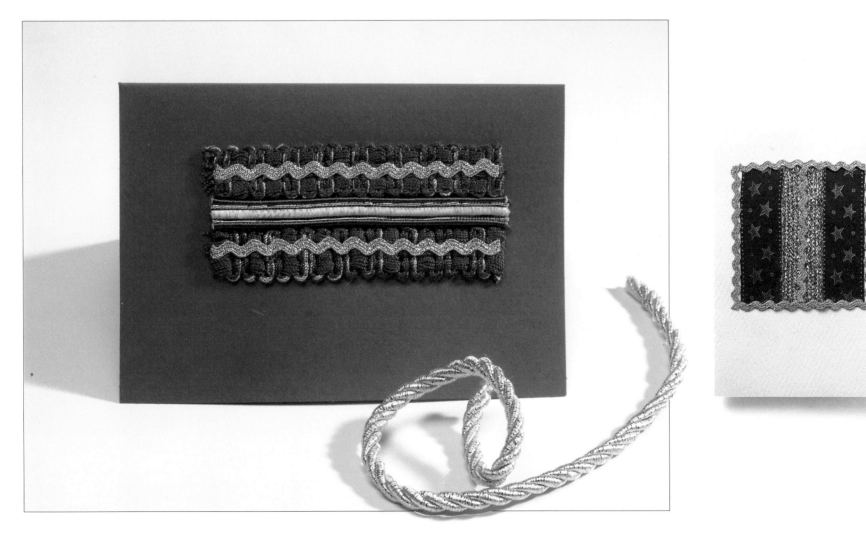

MONOPRINTING

With this easy-to-master technique you can create "one-off" prints. For this project we have used a sun and moon motif which could be suitable for a Birthday card. Any linear designs are appropriate for monoprinting. The exciting element of this technique is surprise – you do not know exactly how the print will turn out until you peel back the paper!

You will need

◊ Black block printing ink
◊ Sheet of glass (4¼ × 6¼in)
◊ HB pencil
◊ White sugar paper (8¼ × 11½in)
◊ Ink rollers, 2⅛in
◊ Large size maroon card blank, 6 × 8in
◊ Strong clear adhesive
◊ Silver colored card
◊ Silver fineline marker pen

1 Place a small amount of ink onto a glass surface and spread it evenly using rollers. It is better to start with too little ink and add more than start with too much.

2 Carefully place a piece of paper onto the inked surface. Using a pencil draw out the design. Remember that your actual print will be the reverse of what is drawn. You can experiment with the pressure applied to the pencil when drawing which will give you darker or lighter lines.

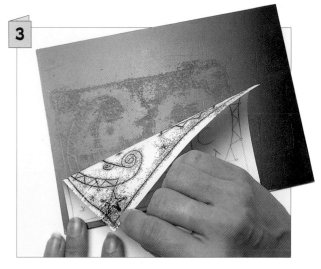

3 When the design is complete, carefully peel back the paper to reveal the print. Leave to dry for approximately 20 minutes.

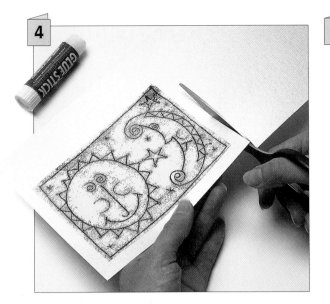

4 When the print is dry, glue it onto a background of silver card and trim to size, leaving a ½–¾in border.

5 Further decoration can be added to the print by "scoring" patterns into the surface of the silver card with a sharp pencil.

6 Finally glue the print onto a larger, folded, contrasting card and draw a border round the card with a silver pen to complete.

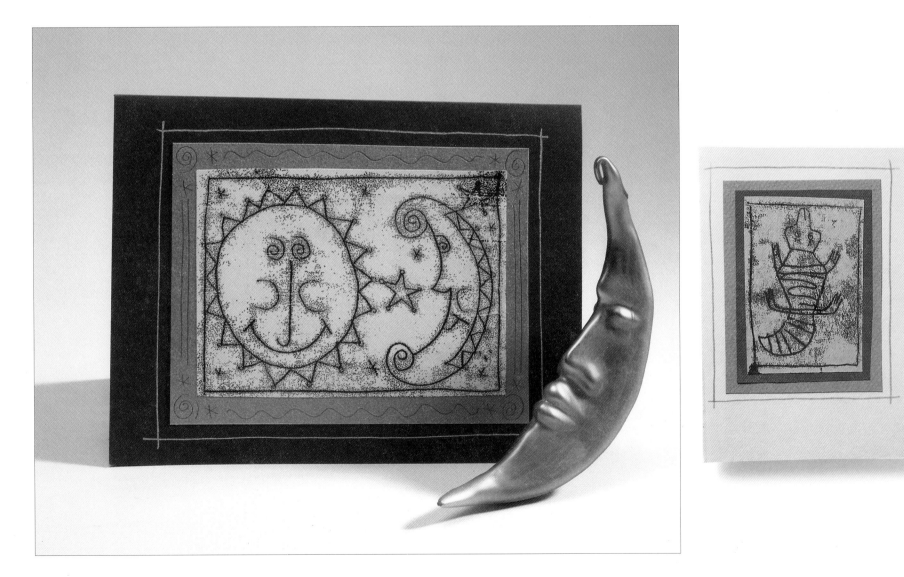

WAX RESIST

A very simple technique is used in this project to produce a greeting card suitable for someone moving to a new home. A naive, child-like illustration of a house creates an effective image.

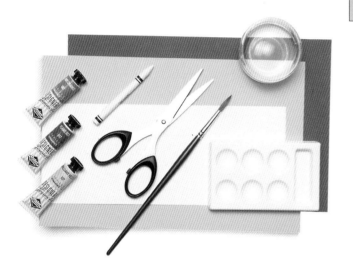

You will need
◊ White wax crayon or candle
◊ Scissors
◊ Watercolor paper
◊ Gouache paint; orange, red and yellow colors
◊ Water pot
◊ Paint brush, size no. 7
◊ Palette
◊ Red or yellow card; 5 × 12in

1 Draw out your design onto watercolor paper using a candle or white wax crayon. The wax can be seen if you tilt the paper into the light.

2 Take a brush loaded with paint and apply it to the paper. It is a good idea to limit the number of colors used to two or three as you can mix them on the paper to create additional shades.

TIP

• It is better to stick to simple motifs for this project such as flowers, hearts, or animals.

---

3 Blend the paints together on the paper using a clean brush and water. Then leave it to dry for approximately 10–20 minutes.

4 Apply a strong glue to the back of the watercolor paper and stick it onto a longer, contrasting piece of card.

5 Fold the card to complete.

RUBBINGS

Once you have made your "master" design almost limitless rubbings can be made from the original. This technique requires very little equipment and the effects of the rubbing can be varied by using different colored wax crayons. The turtle design shown here was inspired by Australian Aboriginal Art.

You will need

◊ Sheet of white sugar or cartridge paper, 8¼ × 11⅛in
◊ Wax crayons; purple and blue color
◊ Sheet of thin detail paper, 8¼ × 11⅛in
◊ Maroon card; 9¼ × 6¼in
◊ Paper cutting scissors
◊ Pencils, 4B and HB
◊ Tracing paper
◊ Glue stick

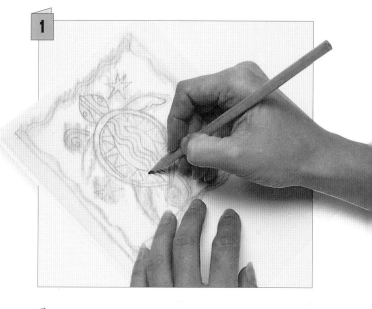

1 Transfer the design onto paper, as described on page 12.

2 Take a pair of scissors and carefully cut out the main sections of the motif.

3

3 Paste the cut-out sections of the design onto a clean sheet of paper.

4

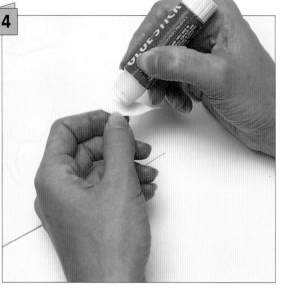

4 Cut out and stick down the decorative elements such as the border, stars and swirls.

5

5 Using a wax crayon and some thin detail paper, rub over the surface. Make sure that the paper is free from any unwanted scraps of paper. Further colors can be added with successive rubbings.

6

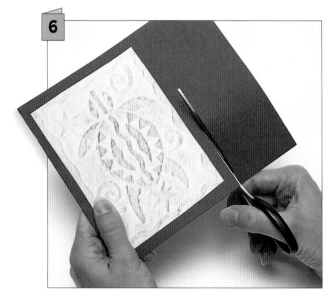

6 Trim the detail paper to size if necessary and glue onto a larger piece of contrasting colored card. Fold this to form a greeting card and cut to size.

CARDS USING METAL

A unique method of recycling your aluminum drinks cans. Linear or punched patterns can easily be created in the soft aluminum giving an embossed effect. Here we have used a simple bird motif which was inspired by American Fold Art. We have then window mounted the metal with card.

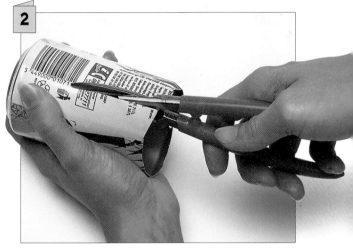

You will need

◊ An aluminum drinks can
◊ Metal tinsnips
◊ Metal scriber
◊ Wire wool
◊ Black fineline fiber-tip pen
◊ Scissors
◊ Double-sided tape
◊ Metal rule
◊ Cutting mat
◊ Mounting board – dark blue; 3 × 3½in
◊ White card blank, 6 × 8in
◊ Craft knife

TIP

• You may want to wear gloves when cutting the can as the edges are quite sharp.

1 Carefully pierce the can using a metal scriber and insert the tinsnips into the hole. Cut off the top of the can.

2 Slit it down the side and remove the base. Once opened out, trim off any uneven edges and cut off a section of metal to work with.

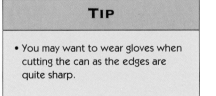

3 Draw out the design onto the reverse (colored side) of the metal using a fiber-tip pen. Do not use a ballpoint pen to draw the design as this will mark the metal surface. Leave at least a ⅛in surround and carefully scribe the design.

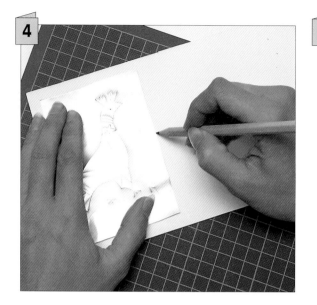

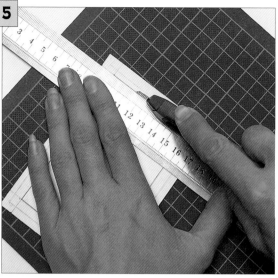

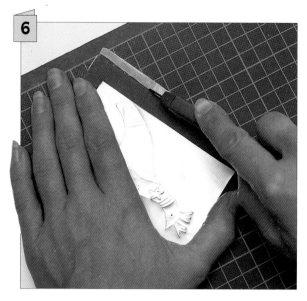

4 When you have completed the scribing, rub over the surface of the metal with wire wool, trim to size if necessary. Place the metal onto a piece of thick cardboard and draw a line around it. This cardboard will form the mount for the metal.

5 Measure and then draw in a border, then draw a third line at least ¼in inside the first to enable the mount to hold the metal in place.

6 Cut along the outside line on the cardboard, and then cut out the center piece of the card.

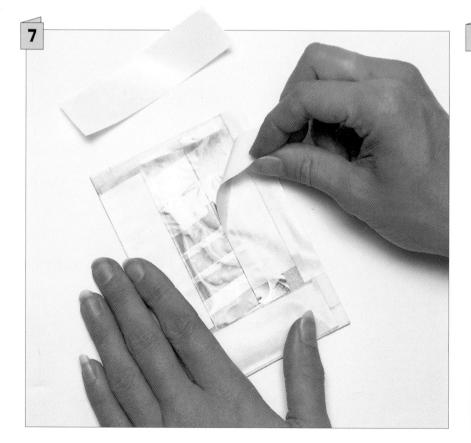

7 Place double-sided tape over the reverse side of the metal and mount. This is more suitable than glue as the metal has a springy quality which makes it difficult for glue to adhere to the surface. Peel back the tape covering and stick them onto a larger, contrasting card. Fold.

8 Small decorative dots on the mount, made with a silver pen, complete the card.

FABRIC COLLAGE

This project illustrates making a greeting card for Valentine's Day or a special card for a loved one.
Using scrap fabrics collected together with the theme colors such as pinks, reds, oranges and golds
to create a very rich, striking effect.

You will need
◊ Pink and red colored felt fabric (small pieces
  6 × 6in)
◊ Gold and woven multi-colored fabric
◊ Fabric scissors
◊ Sewing needle
◊ Red and orange cotton thread
◊ Cotton ball
◊ Paper cutting scissors
◊ PVA adhesive
◊ Old paint brush
◊ White card blank, 6 x 8in
◊ HB pencil
◊ White sugar paper, 2¾ × 2¾in
◊ Gold fineline marker pen

1 Draw out a heart shape on paper then cut it out. Use this as a template.

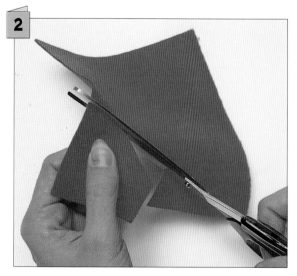

2 Lie the template on the felt and cut out a heart from the fabric.

3 Sew the heart onto a different colored background fabric using a simple running stitch. Do not join up the stitching, instead leave a gap of around ¾in.

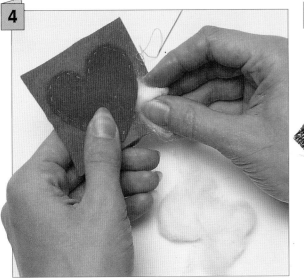

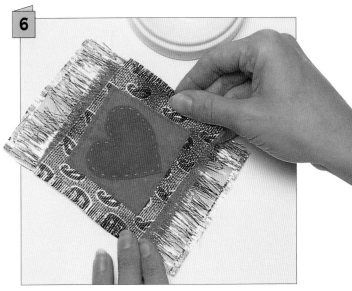

4 Push a small amount of cotton ball through this gap into the heart and sew up the opening. This stuffing will give the heart a 3D effect.

5 Select a larger piece of contrasting fabric to back the felt holding the heart motif, cut it to size and sew them together.

6 If the fabric is quite fine, like the one shown here, deliberately fray the edges to give a decorative effect. As a border, repeat the felt used for the heart. Cut to size and glue it onto the edges of the contrasting frayed fabric.

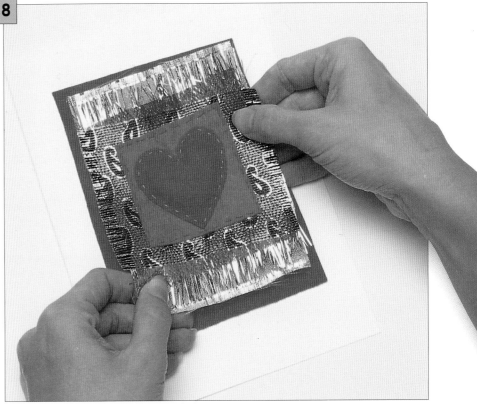

7 Finally glue the collage onto a background layer of the felt to complete. Leave to dry for 50–60 minutes.

8 Once it is dry, glue the completed collage onto a piece of larger, contrasting, folded card.

STAMPING

It is possible to make stamping tools from a variety of materials such as card, potato or sponge. For this project we have used corks, which unlike potato will not deteriorate with time allowing many repeat prints to be made. This particular design is for a Wedding card. The stamped patterns form a circle which is symbolic of fidelity and perpetual renewal.

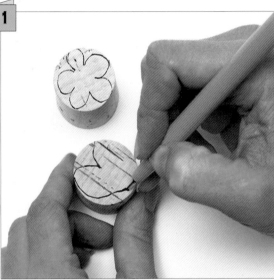

You will need

◊ 2 Champagne corks
◊ White gouache paint
◊ Silver ink
◊ Saucer or palette
◊ Black fiber-tip pen
◊ Scalpel
◊ Sheet of blue sugar paper, 8¼ × 11½in
◊ White card blank, 4 × 6in
◊ Silver fineline marker pen

1 Draw out your chosen motifs onto pieces of cork using a pen.

2 With a scalpel carefully remove the areas surrounding the motifs, so that they stand out from the rest of the cork.

TIP

• Wedding dates or names could be incorporated into the design or a photograph could be pasted into the center of the circle.

3 Draw a circle onto the paper you intend to print upon. You could draw around something such as a jar for this. The circle you have drawn will act as a guide for the stamped pattern.

4 Place some white paint and silver ink onto a palette or saucer. Dip one of the cork stamps into the paint, and the other into the ink and carefully apply the stamps, in turn, to the paper surface along the inside edge of the drawn circle. When the circle of stamps is complete allow the paint to dry for about 10 minutes.

5 Add any further details to the pattern with a silver pen. Finally glue the pattern to a folded, contrasting piece of card.

PAINT STENCILS

For this project we produce another type of stencil, using acetate rather than cardboard. This allows more complex designs, with finer detail, to be cut. The motif used here is a crocodile design inspired by Australian Aboriginal Art. We have used earthy colors to represent those natural pigments used by the native Australians. This type of stencil can be used numerous times and will last longer than a card stencil.

You will need

◊ Sheet of acetate, 8¼ × 11⅛in
◊ Black fiber-tip pen
◊ Scalpel
◊ Masking tape
◊ Red and orange gouache paint
◊ Palette or saucer
◊ Stencil brush
◊ Paint brush (No. 7)
◊ Colored pencils; red, orange, brown, yellow
◊ Cutting mat
◊ Orange and dark brown Ingres paper 3⅛ × 7¾in
◊ Cream card 7¾ x 3in

TIP

• Stencil paints can be obtained from art stores, however it tends to be expensive. We found gouache or latex paint to be just as effective.

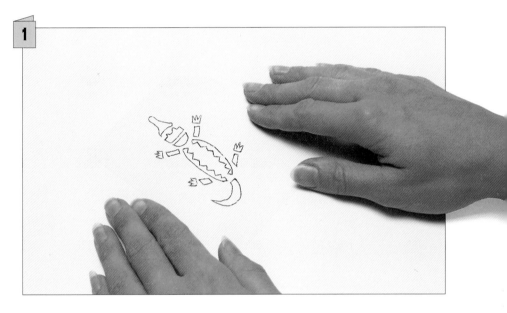

1 Transfer design onto acetate by tracing the template with a fiber-tip pen.

2 Using a scalpel, carefully remove the dark sections of the stenciled template. When you have finished, remove any ink left on the surface of the acetate with a damp tissue.

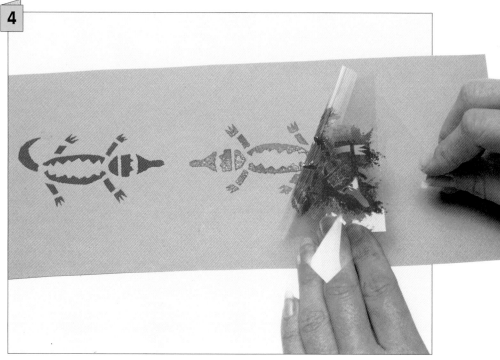

3 Secure the acetate stencil to your chosen paper with masking tape to prevent it slipping. Apply gouache paint over the whole of the stencil using a stencil brush.

4 Remove the masking tape and carefully peel back the stencil, leaving a print of the design. Repeat the process to obtain further prints. Leave to dry for 20–30 minutes.

5 Carefully tear the paper to size and add any further decoration with colored pencils to complete the design.

6 To highlight the torn edge of the paper and create a border, apply a small amount of paint to the edges with a paint brush.

7

8

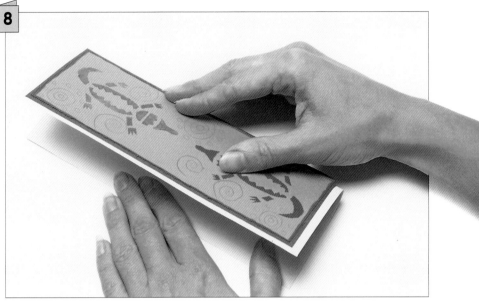

7 When the print is dry glue it to a contrasting colored background and cut to size, leaving a narrow margin round the painted border of the print.

8 Glue this onto a larger piece of card and fold to complete.

BROWN PAPER TECHNIQUE

This is a technique discovered while experimenting with inks and brown parcel paper. You can produce "one-off" pictures or color copy your originals to make multiples of the same design. The card shown in the project has a baby motif which could be used to celebrate the birth of a child.

You will need

◊ Piece of brown parcel paper, 3 × 3in
◊ Black fineline fiber-tip pen
◊ Black water-soluble marker pen
◊ HB pencil
◊ Garden water spray
◊ Paper towel/tissue
◊ Glue stick
◊ Gold fineline marker pen
◊ Cream card blank, 4 × 6in

1 Having drawn your design first in pencil on brown paper, go over it with a fineline permanent black pen.

2 Draw a frame around the design then fill in the area between the frame and the design with a water-soluble marker pen.

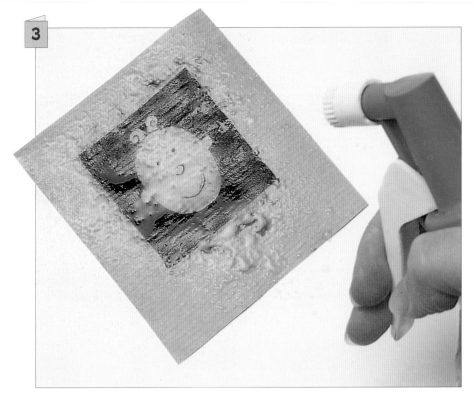

3 Using a water spray, mist over the picture with water. The image will "bleed" around the edges.

4 Dab off any excess water with a paper towel, then leave to dry for approximately 20 minutes.

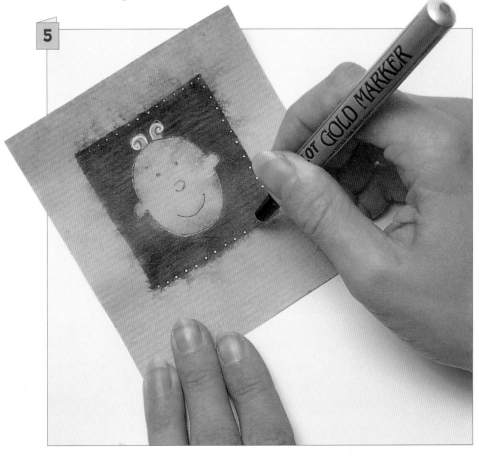

5 Add any further decoration or highlights with a gold pen.

6 Trim to size and glue directly onto a larger, contrasting piece of folded card.

PAPER COLLAGE

This creative painting technique is used to produce rich backgrounds on which to build layers of different papers. The end result being an unusual and individual greeting card. Collect foil papers, Christmas wrapping paper or metallic tissue paper for this project. Choose your paint colors to complement the foil. Here we have used a rich purple and turquoise.

1 Tear up a household sponge into small pieces, so that you can use one piece per color.

You will need
◊ Sheet of watercolor paper, 8¼ × 11⅛in
◊ Sponge
◊ Water spray
◊ Gouache paint; turquoise, ultra-marine, purple
◊ Gold ink
◊ Paint brush no. 7
◊ HB pencil
◊ Steel ruler
◊ Scissors
◊ Various foil papers
◊ Piece of gold card, 2¼ × 2¼in
◊ White card blank, 6 x 8in

TIP

• To obtain a neat torn edge, tear paper against the edge of a ruler.

2 Having selected your paint colors, place them on a palettte or saucer. Mist the watercolor paper with water, then apply the paint to the paper using the pieces of sponge.

3 Mist the painted surface with water again and use a clean piece of sponge to blend the colors together.

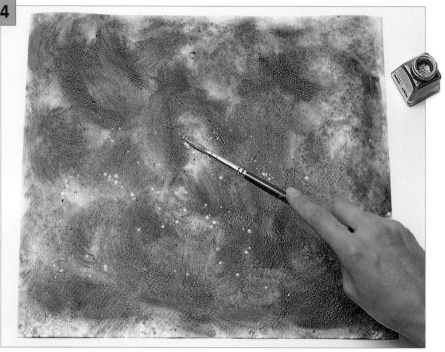

4 Tap a paint brush loaded with gold ink over the surface of the paint to give a "stippled" effect and leave it to dry for 20–30 minutes.

5 Select different color foil papers, cut to required sizes and then crumple them in your hands.

6 Glue these layers together, the largest at the bottom and then in decreasing sizes. First, a large piece of the painted paper which has been torn to size, then the different foil papers and finally a small piece of the painted paper.

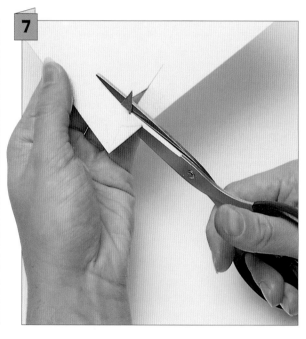

7 Draw a small star onto a piece of gold card, cut it out and then stick it into the center of the collage.

8 Glue the finished collage onto a larger contrasting card. Fold, then draw a gold border with a pen to complete the greeting card.

TIP

• You could use candy wrappers, aluminum foil, etc.

NATURAL PRINTS AND STENCILS

A wide variety of designs can be produced using either natural prints or stencils on their own.
For this project we have combined the two techniques to create an effective leaf motif card.

You will need

◊ A leaf; any fairly flat leaf will do
◊ Red gouache paint
◊ Palette or saucer
◊ Gold ornamental spray
◊ Paper cutting scissors
◊ Paint brush No. 7
◊ Glue stick
◊ Sheets of red and pale cream/green sugar
   paper, 8¼ × 11½in
◊ Cream card blank, 6 × 8in
◊ Gold fineline marker pen

1 Choose a suitable leaf then trim off the stalk if required. Paint the under-side of the leaf, using red gouache paint, where the veins are most prominent.

2 Place the leaf onto a sheet of paper with the painted side facing upward. Put another piece of paper on top of the leaf and press down. Rub over the whole area.

3 Carefully peel back the top sheet of paper to reveal the print. This process can be repeated several times if required.

4 For the background; select several leaves of the same type and place at random onto a sheet of paper. Secure the leaves with a piece of tape on the under-side to prevent them moving when spraying. Spray over the leaves in a "spray booth". Leave to dry for 5 minutes.

5 When dry carefully remove the leaves from the paper.

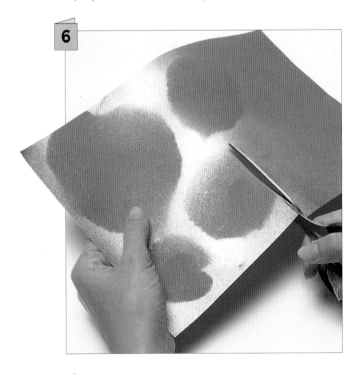

6 Cut the background to size and glue onto a larger, folded piece of contrasting card.

7 Tear the leaf print to size and decorate the torn edges with gold pen.

8 Glue the leaf print onto the sprayed background to complete.

ENVELOPES

It is quite simple to produce your own envelopes. You may want to use a particular type of paper or a shade to match a card. For this project we have chosen a natural color paper to complement the card made with the Brown Paper Technique (page 37).

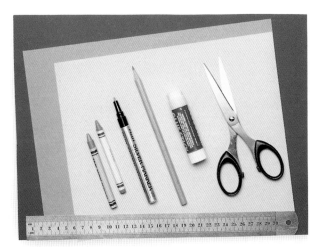

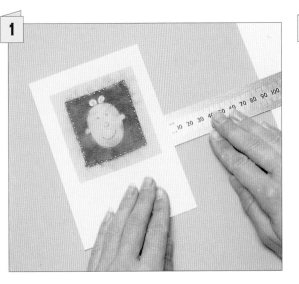

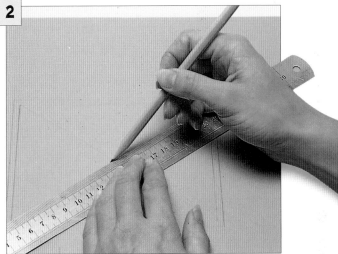

You will need
◊ HB pencil
◊ Paper cutting scissors
◊ Steel ruler
◊ Glue stick
◊ Sheet of paper to match the card, 11¾ × 16⅛in
◊ Wax crayons or silver/gold pens to decorate the envelope

1 Place the card you intend making the envelope for on the chosen paper. Measure around the card allowing a ¼in surrounding space, and draw in the lines.

2 Mark the center of your drawing with a cross, measuring from the four corners.

3 Measure from the center cross to the edge of the top and the edge of the bottom sections. Add this measurement plus ½in for the overlap and make a mark. Draw lines from the corners to these marks to form envelope flaps.

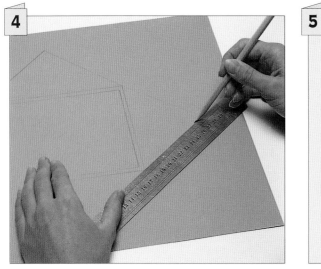

4 Repeat the process for the side flaps but do not add the extra ⅛in.

5 Cut out this finished shape then fold in the flaps to form an envelope.

6 Apply a small amount of glue to the edges of the bottom flap, fold it over and stick it down over the side flaps.

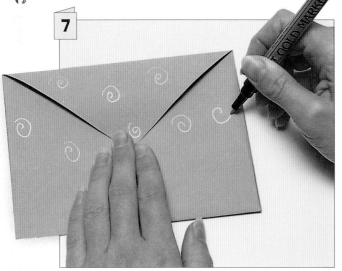

7 The envelope can then be decorated with gold pen as shown, or you can use cork stamps, stencils, etc. to complement the card enclosed.

SUPPLIERS

ARTISTS' SUPPLIES

Winsor & Newton Ltd
51 Rathbone Place
London W1
0171 636 4231

London Graphic Centre
Unit 9–10 McKay Trading Estate
Kensal Road
London W10 5BN
0181 969 6644

Papersource Inc
730 N Franklin Suite 111
Chicago
Illinois, 60610
USA

Sam Flax
111 8th Avenue
New York
NY 10011
(212) 620-3060

PAPERS

Paperchase
213 Tottenham Court Road
London W1P 9AF
0171 580 8496

Falkiner Fine Paper
76 Southampton Row
London NC1B 4AR
0171 831 1151

Paper Art Company
7240 Shadeland Station
Suite 300
Indianapolis IN 46256
(800) 428-5017

Decorative Papers
P O Box 749
Easthampton
MA 01027
(413) 527-6103

CARDS AND ENVELOPES

Craft Creations Ltd
Units 1–7 Harpers Yard
Ruskin Road
Tottenham
London N17 8QA
0181 885 2655

The Cutting Edge
Dept 12B, Unit 14
CEC
Coppull
Lancashire PR7 5AN
01257 792025

Published by Chartwell Books
A Division of Book Sales, Inc.
114 Northfield Avenue
Edison, New Jersey 08837

ISBN 0-7858-0611-3

This book was designed and produced by
Quintet Publishing Limited
6 Blundell Street
London N7 9BH

Creative Director: Richard Dewing
Designer: James Lawrence
Project Editor: Diana Steedman
Editor: Gail Dixon-Smith
Photographer: Paul Forrester

Typeset in Great Britain by
Central Southern Typesetters, Eastbourne
Manufactured in Singapore by Eray Scan Pte Ltd
Printed in China by Leefung-Asco Printers Ltd